DMZ

FREE STATES RISING

BRIAN WOOD WRITER

RICCARDO BURCHIELLI
SHAWN MARTINBROUGH (PARTS ONE & TWO) ARTISTS

JEROMY COX COLORIST

JARED K. FLETCHER LETTERER

COVER BY **BRIAN WOOD**

ORIGINAL SERIES COVERS BY **JOHN PAUL LEON**
DMZ CREATED BY **BRIAN WOOD** AND **RICCARDO BURCHIELLI**

Will Dennis Editor - Original Series **Mark Doyle** Associate Editor - Original Series
Ian Sattler Director - Editorial, Special Projects and Archival Editions
Robin Wildman Editor **Robbin Brosterman** Design Director - Books
Robbie Biederman Publication Design

Karen Berger Senior VP - Executive Editor, Vertigo **Bob Harras** VP - Editor-in-Chief

Diane Nelson President **Dan DiDio** and **Jim Lee** Co-Publishers **Geoff Johns** Chief Creative Officer
John Rood Executive VP - Sales, Marketing and Business Development **Amy Genkins** Senior VP - Business and Legal Affairs **Nairi Gardiner** Senior VP - Finance
Jeff Boison VP - Publishing Operations **Mark Chiarello** VP - Art Direction and Design **John Cunningham** VP - Marketing **Terri Cunningham** VP - Talent Relations and Services
Alison Gill Senior VP - Manufacturing and Operations **David Hyde** VP - Publicity **Hank Kanalz** Senior VP - Digital **Jay Kogan** VP - Business and Legal Affairs, Publishing
Jack Mahan VP - Business Affairs, Talent **Nick Napolitano** VP - Manufacturing Administration **Sue Pohja** VP - Book Sales
Courtney Simmons Senior VP - Publicity **Bob Wayne** Senior VP - Sales

Logo and front cover designed by Brian Wood.

DMZ: FREE STATES RISING
Published by DC Comics. Cover and compilation Copyright © 2012 Brian Wood and Riccardo Burchielli. All Rights Reserved. Originally published in single magazine form in DMZ 60-66 Copyright © 2011
Brian Wood and Riccardo Burchielli. All Rights Reserved. VERTIGO is a trademark of DC Comics. All characters, their distinctive likenesses and related elements featured in this publication are trademarks of
DC Comics. The stories, characters and incidents featured in this publication are entirely fictional. DC Comics does not read or accept unsolicited ideas, stories or artwork.

DC Comics, 1700 Broadway, New York, NY 10019. A Warner Bros. Entertainment Company. Printed in the USA. 2/24/12. First Printing. ISBN: 978-1-4012-3389-1

SUSTAINABLE
FORESTRY
INITIATIVE ·

Certified Sourcing
www.sfiprogram.org
SFI-01042
APPLIES TO TEXT STOCK ONLY

SKREEEEEE

beedle deedle dee

HELLO? YEAH.

NO, YOU FUCKING COME CLOSER.

YOU BRING IT?

IN THE TRUCK.

GET IT.

FIGURE IT'S BETTER JUST TO SWAP VEHICLES RATHER THAN MOVING THE WEAPONS IN THE OPEN.

BORDER PATROL'S GOT DRONES IN THE AREA.

WELL, SHIT.

THAT'S A BRAND NEW PRIUS.

...scenes from the G8 summit currently under way in Phoenix, Arizona, with thousands of protestors in bloody conflict with exhausted police officers.

This is the third week the summit's been delayed due to security concerns, with several international delegations held, quite literally, prisoner within their hotel suites...

...some calling it the "slow death of urban America," dozens more blocks of Richmond, Virginia have been abandoned by municipal authorities, with all utilities, 911, and public transit services withdrawn due to massive budget cuts.

Richmond joins a long list of other cities suffering similar fates. Entire neighborhoods have been reduced to ghost towns in parts of St. Louis, Chicago, Portland, Boston, and Miami...

...latest in a seemingly endless string of police actions, the USS George Washington carrier strike group moves within fifty miles of the horn of Africa, a part of the world all too familiar with American military intervention.

With close to three-quarters of a million troops on the ground in the Middle East, Congress is faced with the largest war funding bill in U.S. history, one expected to pass unanimously...

...like this incident from last week, showing the President barely making it aboard Air Force One. The Secret Service has their hands full with numerous threats every time the President makes a public appearance...

...not to mention the now-common practice of assault weapons carried in public. Massive resistance from the NRA and politicians on the Hill have tied law enforcement's hands...

...scenes like this from Fort Conrad, where dozens if not hundreds of bodies of fallen soldiers sit out in the rain, unclaimed and unidentified. Repeated calls to military command have gone unanswered, and the residents of the town are faced with the horrifying thought of having to open the coffins and identify the bodies themselves...

...in an Op Ed article in today's *Times,* decried the administration's clear lack of domestic agenda, noting that fear-mongering and constantly playing the "homeland defense" card is accomplishing nothing but a further disintegration of the fabric of American society.

With a combined thirty-nine years of war on no less than six fronts across the globe, he goes on to wonder "Just what is it that defines us these days? What does America mean – not only to the rest of the world – but to us at home?"

Got a tip about the Minot AFB... like so many others, it's flush with Homeland Security funding but something like 90% of the staff is on deployment.

You can just walk in and take whatever isn't nailed down.

WE'RE TAKING SIDE ROADS, SKIRTING THE BASE, SO WE'LL COME IN FROM THE NORTH...

Half the country seems out to lunch. Dead towns, empty streets, closed signs everywhere you look.

...THIS AIN'T THE MOVIES, OR AFGHANISTAN. WE WALK IN, PUT GUNS ON THE GUARDS, AND LOAD UP THE TRUCKS. THAT'S IT.

I'LL DROP YOU GUYS OFF BACK IN TOWN, GIVE YOU ANOTHER $10K EACH, COOL?

WHO THE FUCK ARE YOU CALLING?

WIFE.

I'LL BE LATE, GIMME A BREAK.

The closest thing resembling the law out here's the ATF, and they're more like mafia than anything else.

...unknown substance found in this peaceful suburbs mail system this morning. At least seven carriers suspected to have been exposed...

...latest in a rash of school bombings that seem to have one thing in common – all serving affluent counties with representatives who voted for the recent round of Pentagon war funding...

...negotiations having run out, New York City SWAT teams move in on City Hall Park.

...another sighting of the ominous split-star image that some claim belongs to a new political party starting to form in America's heartland. No official announcement has been made, but rumors of its intent range from a benign student peace movement to nothing less than a violent insurgent army

DMZ

FREE STATES RISING

THE UNITED STATES OF AMERICA.

MONTHS LATER.

...absolute carnage stretching across four states as elements of the so-called "Free States Army" continue their push east. Residents of the Mid-Atlantic states brace themselves for the arrival of what is, truly, a second American civil war...

...so far have put forward no leader or public position. Estimates range from four to sixteen different "FSA" Army elements on the move, each one its own front in this very unconventional conflict...

...described as "ripe for the picking," National Guard bases continue to fall and be absorbed by "Free States" insurgents, picking armories clean in the process. Reports that National Guard soldiers are defecting to the rebel ranks remain unverified.

...complete and total silence following the Presidential address...

From Fort Lee to Bayonne, we have men and vehicles. The Turnpike's a fucking parking lot. I don't know how many people they got in the city right now, but my gut tells me we probably got pretty equal numbers.

Every day, maybe every hour, they got C-130's landing at JFK and La Guardia, troops coming back from overseas to reinforce the city. I hear people around me congratulating themselves at forcing the end of some of these foreign wars...

...like that's the point of what we're doing. Like that'll be the END of it.

Like those troops won't be doing anything about us.

Talk about a fucking POLICE ACTION.

DUDE.

WANNA GO INVADE A CITY?

...a defiant city to the end, a metropolis having endured too much in the past, destined to be yet another symbol in this increasingly violent and fractured world. Tonight, as the city goes dark, as Con Ed pulls the plug on the grid, a moment of silence is observed...

It looks so close I feel like I could touch it.

This isn't how it ends for me.

CLICK

COVER ME!

VIP VIP VIP VIP

Not in a fucking tunnel.

SPINK SPINK FWIP FWIP

CHAK CHAK

GET READY TO ADVANCE!

GET THESE GUYS TO FIND THE PUMPS, GET THE TUNNEL CLEARED OF WATER. THEN SET UP ANOTHER CHECKPOINT ON THE JERSEY SIDE.

THE JERSEY SIDE?

WE FOUGHT FOR THIS TUNNEL...

...WE'RE KEEPING IT.

PEOPLE CAN START LISTENING TO ME FOR A CHANGE.

Once an army, then a movement, most recently a clusterfuck.

Time for the Free States to be an army again. It starts here.

New York City.

MANHATTAN.
THE DMZ.
THE UNITED STATES OF AMERICA.

TWO NIGHTS AGO.

HEY HEY, LOOK WHO IT IS.

THE "PRESS."

For the last thirty hours, bombs have fallen on the island of Manhattan. That doesn't sound like anything new, but what if I told you more tonnage fell in that one time frame than in the last half-decade of the war?

With the world finally and unequivocally on their side, the United States government finally opened the stockpiles.

And to think the real battle has yet to be fought. I've heard it called a few things in the last couple hours: "The Liberation of Manhattan," "The Battle for Broadway," "The Push to the End," etc. etc.

I'm sure it has a proper name, something along the lines of "Operation: United Homeland," maybe. But everyone knows what's really about to happen.

If the city of New York is the door that leads to the Free States Army...

We're about to kick it down on our way through.

THIS IS HOW I SEE IT, ROTH, AND YOU CORRECT ME IF I'M WRONG...

YOUR BASIC FUNCTION HERE IS TO KEEP AN EYE ON US... LIKE SOME KIND OF MEDIA WATCHDOG. RIGHT?

LET ME TELL YOU WHAT *I'M* HERE FOR.

YOU PROBABLY HAVE THIS IDEA THAT I'M SOME KIND OF WARMONGER. TRUTH IS, I DIDN'T WANT THIS POSTING. "COMMANDER, U.S. FORCES MANHATTAN"? IT'S A *MINEFIELD*, BEST CASE SCENARIO.

THIS IS AN UGLY WAR AND IT'S ONLY GOING TO GET UGLIER BEFORE IT'S OVER. WHICH'LL BE *SOON*, NOW, BUT I'M NEVER GOING TO BE ABLE TO WASH THE DIRT OFF.

I'LL ALWAYS BE THE GUY THAT DESTROYED NEW YORK CITY. THIS IS THE LAST COMMAND I'M EVER GOING TO HAVE.

DON'T YOU RETIRED GUYS ALWAYS END UP MAKING A KILLING AS LIBERTY NEWS EXPERTS?

FUNNY, ROTH, CONSIDERING.

YEAH, BUT I'M NOT DOING THIS FOR LIBERTY NEWS. YOU KNOW WHY I'M HERE.

YOU'RE A NECESSARY EVIL. *NO OFFENSE*, OF COURSE.

LOOK, I *GET IT*, ROTH. I DO. YOU'RE THE EYES AND THE EARS THAT'LL LEGITIMIZE THIS VICTORY IN THE COURT OF WORLD OPINION. I GET THAT.

I FUCKING *HATE* IT, BUT I GET IT.

US ARMY

CLEAR THROUGH TO THE BOWERY, AND NORTH TO EAST FOURTH, EAST FIFTH. QUIET NIGHT OUT THERE, COPY?

COPY THAT. MAINTAIN YOUR GRID.

LISTEN UP! WE HAVE A GO. TEAM A, MOVE EAST TO THE BOWERY I WANT A FULL RECON REPORT BY 0500 HOURS.

ROTH'LL GO WITH YOU.

It was a tense room.

No one had any clue what was out there.

HEY, HEY ROTH...!

YOU KNOW THIS STREET?

WALKED IT A HUNDRED TIMES, WHY?

SHUT UP!

FUCK THIS. THIS CANYON IS A DEATHTRAP.

WE'RE HEADING TO HIGH GROUND. FOLLOW ME.

ROTH! WHAT THE FUCK!

You just have to give in to it. I remember now.

Took me months to figure out in the first place, but you can't control what happens here. It's gonna happen, what-ever's gonna happen.

It's when you try and force it, that's when people start dying.

I'm here to bear witness to this invasion, and the subsequent occupation and "pacification" of the city of New York. This is such a closed warzone, with zero press coverage, it was deemed necessary that there be one neutral set of eyes and ears on the ground.

I still have mixed feelings about whether I'm the guy for the job, but I'm here and I'm determined not to fuck it up this time.

And in the category of "not fucking it up" I realize that being totally impartial is one thing, but standing by while these soldiers get themselves killed is another.

This invasion is happening, the army's here, and nothing is going to stop any of this. I can't stop any of it.

And if I try and deny that fact, I'm going to get people killed.

Again.

IS THIS ON THE LEVEL, ROTH?

HOW CAN WE BE SURE YOU'RE NOT SENDING US STRAIGHT INTO SOME AMBUSH YOUR DMZ PALS HAVE SET UP?

THAT'S EASY...

"...I DON'T HAVE FRIENDS HERE ANYMORE."

By 0600 hours that morning, the reports were in and the pilots had their targets.

I was mildly startled at the notion that targets still existed. From where I was standing, the city looked deserted.

The strategy was absurdly simple: a slow, methodical, sweep east to west across the island, the Black Hawks clearing lanes for the armor and ground troops.

So far, it's been quiet. The unspoken assumption on everyone's mind was that the enemy (who is the enemy exactly?) is waiting for the army to get midway before closing in from behind and on the flanks.

The only viable counter to that is to overwhelm with sheer numbers.

For the entire length of this war. The U.S. has been recalling troops from overseas. The bridges and tunnels are still crowded with troops entering the city.

So far, nothing at all from the Free States Army.

Why confide in me?

Was it a last ditch effort, sitting in that interrogation room, almost certainly looking at the last hours of his life?

He's always been one step ahead of me, manipulating a certain action or reaction out of me.

No matter what I do, it always manages to serve his ends.

That has to stop.

Can I do this?

Do I have a choice?

...day four of the Battle for Manhattan, as the massive column of American troops continues to pour into the island, its defenders still reeling from the air campaign, offering little to no resistance...

...massive arms caches discovered, foreign-manufactured automatic weapons and ammunition, serial numbers rerportedly filed off. For more speculation on possible countries of origin, we take you to...

...not without risk, and pockets of insurgent activity must still be rooted out. The President, speaking from American Command aboard Air Force One, promised a swift end to this final battle, and a thorough one

...sort of barbarity we have come to associate...

"...this is an operation based on pragmatism rather than emotion," the commander was quoted as saying. "My soldiers are not here to be tourists, and for the duration of this operation, Manhattan is not an American city but a field of battle..."

...almost unprecedented war, pitting a country against itself on an epic scale. It's impossible to predict how history will judge this conflict, but however it does, it will be tinged with a profound sadness that I suspect we've only begun to realize

RRRRRRRRr

CLICK

WHUMP

FUCK!

...MATTY?

WHERE ARE YOU...?

REACH OUT. OPEN THE CURTAINS.

...PARCO?

...a night of fierce fighting perfectly illustrates the dangers lurking in every dark alley and behind every crumbling building in this city...

...while the civilian toll remains a popular topic for debate. U.S. Army spokesmen repeatedly insist that all civilians who wished to be evacuated to safe zones have been kept safe, leaving behind only people dedicated to violence. Critics denounce that as deliberately naïve, that in a city of this size...

...already seeking contract bids for the inevitable rebuilding of infrastructure...

A few days ago I told some soldier that I didn't have any friends left in the city. I meant that...I mean, that's how it feels.

But deep down I knew that, whatever the situation, Wilson had time for me. I don't think we were ever pals, but he never judged me or ever got pissed off at me. Even when I came after his money.

It was the sanest relationship I had with anyone in the DMZ.

Did I ever think, even briefly, that he wouldn't make it through this war?

I don't think I ever did.

He's Wilson.

Listening to this girl, I don't know how well I ever knew him. He had a whole life in this neighborhood, so separate from the rest of the city. All those times we hung out, was that actually Wilson I was with?

Or the fake Wilson he put on for the sake of outsiders?

I'm not going to kid myself that I was anything but an outsider.

Suddenly I'm second-guessing everything.

It's just so inconceivable.

He accomplished so much, had such influence and engendered so much loyalty from everyone around him. And he gave it all up and shipped them across the river into custody.

I feel like I'm missing some part of the puzzle.

CAN I DROP YOU OFF SOMEWHERE?

But then I realize that what I'm really missing--who I'm really missing...

...is Zee.

...begins today, the United States of America vs. Trustwell Incorporated, a private security firm charged with, among other things, the assassination of former U.N. Ambassador Gunnarsson...

..long-awaited settlement was reached today in the matter of PFC Chris Stevens and the wrongful death suit filed by his family. Stevens was charged with – and eventually found innocent of – lethal participation in the day 204 Massacre...

...but not before he was dropped to his death by members of his own unit, allegedly in retaliation for his testimony about that horrific day...

...debuting at number one on both the French and Japanese charts, this is DJ Random Fire...

MANHATTAN
THE DMZ

"...AS THIS 'BATTLE FOR MANHATTAN' HITS ITS APEX, IT'S CLEAR THE U.S. IS THE WINNING SIDE, WITH AN ESTIMATED 75% OF THE CITY FEELING ITS PRESENCE..."

"...IT'S ALSO CLEAR THAT TRADITIONAL OCCUPATION IS NOT THE PLAN *THIS* TIME AROUND. INSTEAD, THE ARMY IS MOVING THROUGH THE STREETS LIKE A STORM, STOMPING ON ANY RESISTANCE IT FINDS *ALMOST* WITHOUT SLOWING DOWN.

"AND THERE'S A *LOT* OF RESISTANCE, SINCE THE PHOTOS OF THE EXECUTED FREE STATES COMMANDER WERE RELEASED TO THE PUBLIC. PART OF THE U.S. STRATEGY IS AIMED AT ANTAGONIZING ANY ENEMY FORCES AND GETTING THEM TO APPEAR OUT IN THE OPEN...

"...THE COMMANDER WAS NOT A PUBLIC FIGURE BY ANY DEFINITION OF THE TERM, BUT SO FEW IN THE FREE STATES' COMMAND STRUCTURE ARE KNOWN, THAT ANYONE IN A LEADERSHIP ROLE IS CONSIDERED 'HIGH VALUE.' TO *BOTH* SIDES, ACTUALLY...

"...THIS IS AN UGLY BATTLE, WHICH IS SAYING SOMETHING ABOUT A CIVIL WAR THAT HAS RAGED FOR CLOSE TO A DECADE. BUT THE U.S. HAS TAKEN ITS SELF-DESCRIBED MANDATE FIRMLY IN HAND AND HAS RUN WITH IT...

"--LITERALLY MOST OF THE TIME--LEVELING A WEAPON IN FRONT TO CLEAR ANY PATH..."

"THIS IS THE *END,* NOW. ASK ANYONE ON THE STREET, OR ANYONE IN UNIFORM. THIS, ALL THIS HAPPENING RIGHT NOW, THIS IS THE END OF THE WAR."

"AND IT'LL BE A DECISIVE END. NO INTERIM GOVERNMENTS OR CEASEFIRES. THE U.S. MILITARY ACTION IS SO HEAVY-HANDED..."

"...AND THE RESISTANCE FROM BOTH THE FREE STATES IRREGULARS, AS WELL AS ANY CIVILIAN CAUGHT IN THE MIX, IS SO INTENSE..."

"THIS IS *IT.* THE U.S. ARMY IS A BOOT GRINDING DOWN..."

"...AND WHEN IT LIFTS ITSELF BACK UP, WHAT WILL BE LEFT INTACT?"

THIS IS AN EXTRAORDINARY MILITARY TRIBUNAL, MR. PARCO, AND SO YOU ARE NOT ENTITLED TO--

THAT WAS A JOKE.

I KNOW WHAT THIS IS.

FINE. NOW, CAN YOU COMMENT ON YOUR TIES TO THE FREE STATES OF AMERICA MOVEMENT, SPECIFICALLY AS THEY PERTAIN TO ARMED AND VIOLENT ATTACKS ON U.S. PERSONNEL, INFRASTRUCTURE, AND INTERESTS?

FOR A PERIOD OF TIME, SOME TWO YEARS BACK, THE FSA WAS SUPPORTING MY ELECTION BID FOR THE OFFICE OF CITY GOVERNOR.

SUPPORTING IN WHAT WAY, SPECIFICALLY?

FINANCIAL, WHEN NECESSARY TO GREASE THE WHEELS. I WAS ALSO PROVIDED A SECURITY DETAIL DESIGNED TO LOOK LOCAL, AND THERE WERE ASSURANCES GIVEN... FOR MY SAKE, I MEAN...

IT WAS CLEAR TO ME I WAS MEANT TO BE THEIR FOOT IN THE DOOR, SO TO SPEAK, BUT I MADE IT EQUALLY CLEAR TO THEM THAT I INTENDED TO ACTUALLY FULFILL THE DUTIES THE OFFICE DEMANDED. I HAD NO INTENTION OF BEING A PUPPET.

ISN'T THAT EXACTLY WHAT THEY WERE ASKING YOU TO BE, THOUGH?

NOT AS I NEGOTIATED IT...

MY PRESENCE AS GOVERNOR WAS MEANT TO CLEAR THE CITY OF THE U.S. MILITARY. ONCE THAT HAPPENED, THEY WOULD DO THEIR THING AND I WOULD BE FREE TO DO MINE.

TO THE FSA, MANHATTAN WAS A SQUARE ON THE CHESS BOARD, TO OCCUPY FOR A MINUTE BEFORE CONTINUING ON TOWARDS THEIR GOAL.

FOR ME, MANHATTAN WAS THE GOAL.

...ARROGANT PRICK...

...

ARE YOU MAKING SOME SORT OF ACCUSATION HERE, MR. DELGADO?

CALL YOUR PRESIDENT.

I HAVE PROOF.

WHERE IS IT?

WELL?

MR. DELGADO?

DO YOU REMEMBER THE VIKTOR FOOTAGE?

KEEPING THAT SECRET, HOLDING THAT IN RESERVE...DID IT DO ANY GOOD IN THE END?

IT KEPT US ALIVE.

IT KEPT *YOU* ALIVE, YOU MEAN.

DID IT END THE WAR ANY FASTER? DID IT MAKE ANY OF THE PLAYERS ACT ANY BETTER? DID IT PREVENT ANY OF THE HORRIBLE SHIT THAT'S GONE DOWN IN THE LAST FIVE YEARS?

WHEN YOU THINK ABOUT GRAND NOTIONS LIKE "THE GREATER GOOD" AND "THE TRUTH," THINK ABOUT WHAT IS TRULY THE *GREATEST* GOOD.

YOU MIGHT BE ABLE TO BOIL A CONFLICT DOWN TO A MORAL ISSUE...

The war isn't over.

But its time has definitely come...

NAME: PARCO DELGADO. TIME OF DEATH, 4:42PM.

...and it doesn't even matter why.

After all these years of chasing down truths, this is a lie I can maintain.

This is a cause worth the deception.

"WHAT THE FUCK'S GOING ON?"

YOU SAY ANOTHER WORD, I'LL KICK ALL YOUR FUCKING TEETH IN.

If nations lie and manipulate to start wars, I can do the same to end one.

PARCO!

HOW...?

WHO CARES.

But what my Dad wouldn't get is that the promise of an end isn't enough.

Even after the last bullet is fired, the last tank turns around, and the ink on the peace deal is dry...

...we have a
city to rebuild.

MARTEL?

FIVE YEARS AGO.

CREEEEK CRIK CRACK

NO, PLEASE...!

I should have listened to my gut.

I should have known this would come to no good.

...

146

=OOF=

WHERE'D YOU COME FROM, KID?

Had to be a good four years younger than me, some stupid kid with too much power and no idea how to use it.

But I'll cut myself a little bit of slack, at least on that first night.

BINGO?

OH YEAH, BINGO.

The IDIOT came bearing gifts.

The more I poked around, the less sense it made.

Who is this guy? Wait, I know the answer to that. He's NO ONE. But here he is, loaded to the hilt with equipment, cash, and communications gear. Supplies, and what looks like broadcast software.

Who knows what else, out in that helicopter.

So, not celebrity.

And not military.

OH, FINE.

I GUESS YOU'VE EARNED IT.

Must be the press.

Or someone desperately trying to be, anyway.

Here you go again, Zee.

Taking in strays.

This one seems useful, I justify to myself.

Worth seeing what he has to say for himself, when he wakes up.

He's probably a little imperialist, like everyone else from across the river.

Come to gawk at the natives.

But, like I said, he's got some power. Clout.

Depending on what he does with it...

...he might SURPRISE me.

149

Upstate's probably FRIED now, anyway.

I take that bit of knowledge and stuff it deep down inside. Where I don't have to think about it much.

THE NEW YORK PUBLIC LIBRARY

I try not to think about ANYTHING too much these days.

His stupid Delgado fixation.

Parco played him. Knowing Matty, I'm not sure he'll ever get over that.

I remember thinking at the time, well, he can have Parco Delgado or he can have me.

Knowing full well who he'd choose, and feeling faintly smug that he'll never truly have either of us.

He had POTENTIAL, that one.

Then he had to start carrying a gun and being Mr. Tough Guy.

But he had potential, the dork...

...even if I was the only one who saw it.

TWO YEARS AGO.

WHAT'S THE MATTER?

WHAT DO YOU MEAN?

YOU'RE SO DISTRACTED.

I'M NOT.

Why did I do it?

I carried Matty's files around with me for weeks, trying to think what to do. Where to put them. I hid them, kept them dry.

He never ONCE made an effort to find me. To come after me.

It was a year since I'd left.

Too busy playing WARLORD with his personal army.

FUCK, ANGEL, DO IT! **DO IT!**

And now he's back, or so I hear.

Matty Roth, just in time to end the war.

They can have each other. I'm DONE.

I've played my part.

I've carried the pain and suffering of this city on my shoulders for too long.

I've borne the brunt of exactly the sort of shit the Roths of the world dish out.

WUFF WUFF WUFF